Danger, Mystery & Adventure

50
CREATIVE
WRITING
PROMPTS

D1783765

Name:

Date:

Address:

Phone:

Email:

Finally, He was going; he was finally backpacking through Europe. He was sitting in the café with his coffee, travel books, and map trying to decide his first destination.

_____
_____
_____
_____
_____
_____
_____
_____
_____
_____
_____
_____
_____
_____
_____
_____
_____
_____
_____
_____

I have lived on this mountain alone for a long time now, ever since that summer when...

_____

_____

_____

_____

_____

_____

_____

_____

_____

_____

_____

_____

_____

_____

_____

_____

_____

_____

_____

_____

_____

_____

They had just hit the open seas, the captain was shouting orders and his crew of pirates hurried to do his bidding. The new cabin boy watched everything with cautious eyes; he hoped no one would discover his secret.

_____
_____
_____
_____
_____
_____
_____
_____
_____
_____
_____
_____
_____
_____
_____
_____
_____

This coming summer, anything is possible! Make your summer bucket list!

_____
_____
_____
_____
_____
_____
_____
_____
_____
_____
_____
_____
_____
_____
_____
_____
_____
_____
_____
_____
_____
_____

You come home to a note on your door saying, "You're in danger, leave this city, but don't tell anyone."

_____

_____

_____

_____

_____

_____

_____

_____

_____

_____

_____

_____

_____

_____

He had been mountain biking for as long as he could remember; there wasn't a trail he couldn't ride, until today...

_____

_____

_____

_____

_____

_____

_____

_____

_____

_____

_____

_____

_____

_____

_____

_____

Make a list of five things you're afraid of happening to you. Write a story in which one of them happens.

_____

_____

_____

_____

_____

_____

_____

_____

_____

_____

_____

_____

_____

_____

_____

_____

The hot air balloons were rising higher and higher at an alarming rate, suddenly a strong wind took hold of the balloons sending them far over the mountains.

_____
_____
_____
_____
_____
_____
_____
_____
_____
_____
_____
_____
_____
_____
_____
_____
_____
_____
_____

Running his hand along the cave wall he mutters, "I KNOW I have seen this symbol before..."

_____

_____

_____

_____

_____

_____

_____

_____

_____

_____

_____

_____

_____

_____

_____

_____

_____

_____

_____

The Stones were massive and cold, ice cold, it gave him chills. The place almost felt as if it was alive, and he thought for sure he was hearing things, it sounded as if noise was coming from the stones, like a rhythm calling to him.

As he swung out over the water he could see his own reflection, he could also see something else that made him hold a little tighter to the rope.

_____
_____
_____
_____
_____
_____
_____
_____
_____
_____
_____
_____
_____
_____
_____
_____
_____
_____
_____
_____
_____
_____
_____

Looking around to make sure he wasn't followed, he stepped into the cave walking out into another world. It was his secret, the cave, not that anyone would believe it.

Sitting on the train a young man is watching out the window as they chugged past endless prairie, a voice breaks through his boredom, "We need to get off this train".

_____
_____
_____
_____
_____
_____
_____
_____
_____
_____
_____
_____
_____
_____
_____
_____
_____

Sitting on the ground I tossed pieces of meat trying to coax the cheetah cub closer. It had been coming around for weeks. Maybe tonight he will finally let me pet him.

_____
_____
_____
_____
_____
_____
_____
_____
_____
_____
_____
_____
_____
_____
_____
_____
_____
_____

They could see the light coming and had been watching it for a while. One lone lantern, heading right toward their campsite! Was it bringing a friendly traveler looking to share their fire, or was it bringing trouble?

_____

_____

_____

_____

_____

_____

_____

_____

_____

_____

_____

_____

_____

_____

_____

_____

The boy had strayed too far from the camp site while gathering wood, he was hurrying to get back, it was getting dark. he could hear the wolves, they were howling early tonight. He hurried a little faster, as he stepped into the clearing he came upon them.

_____

_____

_____

_____

_____

_____

_____

_____

_____

_____

_____

_____

_____

_____

_____

_____

_____

What are the most important things to you in your life?
What would your life be like if just one went missing?

_____
_____
_____
_____
_____
_____
_____
_____
_____
_____
_____
_____
_____
_____
_____
_____
_____
_____
_____
_____

A distant relative gives you one million dollars, and a quest to touch the world with kindness...

_____
_____
_____
_____
_____
_____
_____
_____
_____
_____
_____
_____
_____
_____
_____
_____
_____
_____
_____
_____
_____

The trail was littered with autumn leaves, the colors were brilliant, I almost didn't even see the fox before it stepped out onto the path. "Follow me.."

"What?!" I asked stunned, I must be hearing things. "Follow me... we can't be late."

_____

_____

_____

_____

_____

_____

_____

_____

_____

_____

_____

_____

_____

_____

_____

_____

_____

They had not received any word from his brother in days, his brother had gone to the top of the mountain and he should have been home by now. He decided it was up to him to see if his brother needed help.

_____
_____
_____
_____
_____
_____
_____
_____
_____
_____
_____
_____
_____
_____
_____
_____
_____

Cold, tired, and hungry, the two friends wanted nothing more than to be home. They were in the last stretch of their winter hike. They came across three horses saddled and standing together, no one around, and no footprints in the snow.

_____
_____
_____
_____
_____
_____
_____
_____
_____
_____
_____
_____
_____
_____
_____
_____
_____

Drinking his coffee while watching the fire and cooking breakfast, he could hear his family starting to wake up in their tents. He wondered for a moment what he would be doing right now if he didn't have a family.

_____

_____

_____

_____

_____

_____

_____

_____

_____

_____

_____

_____

_____

_____

_____

_____

_____

It was the opportunity of a lifetime and I knew that this was a moment I would never forget. I'll admit I didn't expect such a long jump! With the Grand Canyon below and the blue sky above, it was my moment to...

_____

_____

_____

_____

_____

_____

_____

_____

_____

_____

_____

_____

_____

_____

_____

_____

_____

_____

_____

It was finally here, his 17th birthday, the day he would receive his very own dragon! He hurried to the cottage, hoping the egg hadn't hatched yet.

_____

_____

_____

_____

_____

_____

_____

_____

_____

_____

_____

_____

_____

_____

_____

_____

_____

_____

_____

I stood outside the door, holding the key in my hand; I just had to unlock it...

_____

_____

_____

_____

_____

_____

_____

_____

_____

_____

_____

_____

_____

_____

_____

_____

_____

_____

_____

_____

_____

I stopped at a fork in the road I just had to choose which way to go.

_____

_____

_____

_____

_____

_____

_____

_____

_____

_____

_____

_____

_____

_____

_____

_____

_____

_____

_____

_____

"What happened?" he asked.

_____
_____
_____
_____
_____
_____
_____
_____
_____
_____
_____
_____
_____
_____
_____
_____
_____
_____
_____
_____
_____

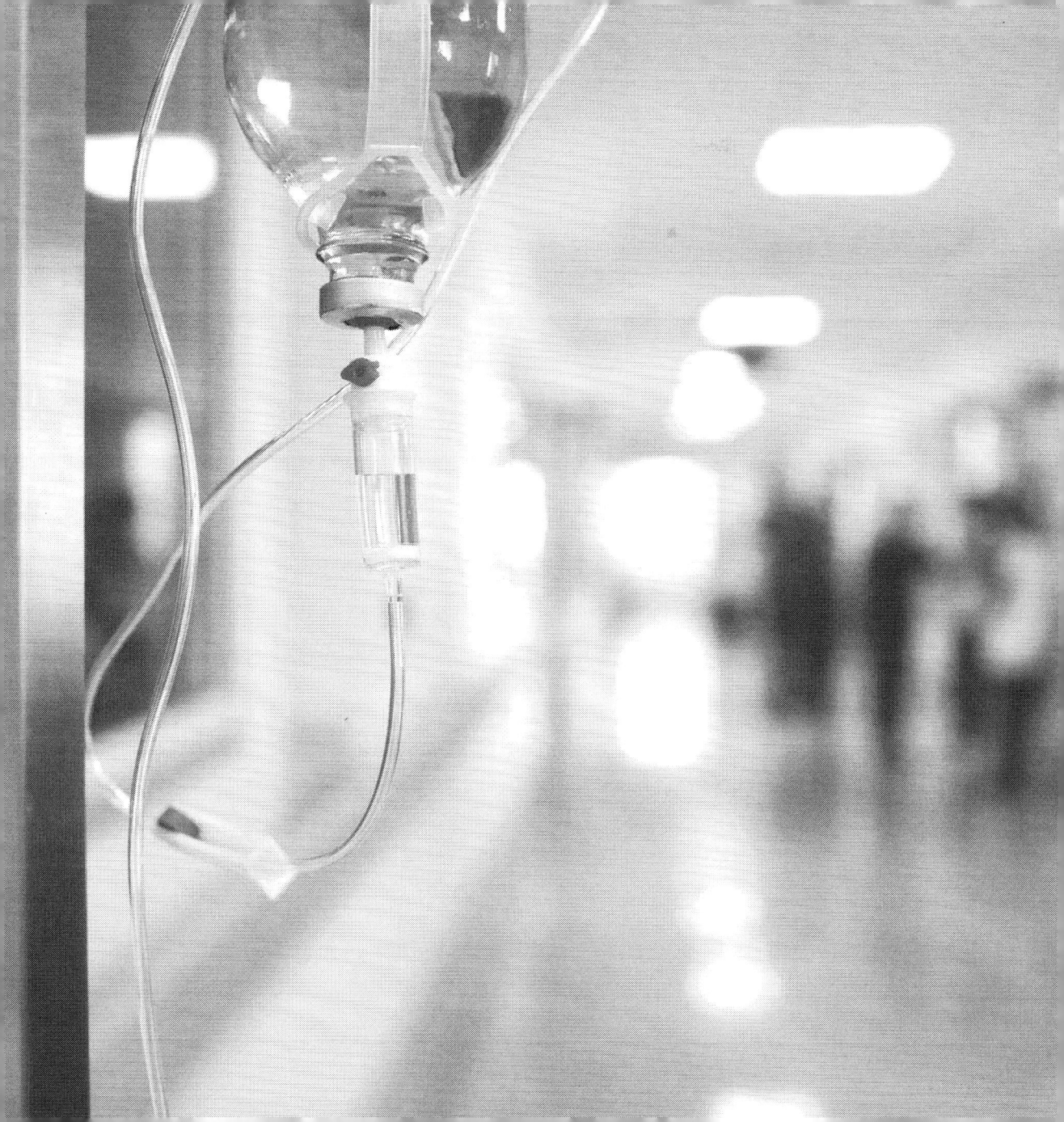

A heart for adventure. A week with the cousins. $27.50 to spend. A bus ride to somewhere. And then the dare...

_____

_____

_____

_____

_____

_____

_____

_____

_____

_____

_____

_____

_____

_____

_____

_____

_____

_____

_____

_____

Write a short letter from your five-year-old self,

and write a letter to your five year old self.

_____
_____
_____
_____
_____
_____
_____
_____
_____
_____
_____

_____
_____
_____
_____
_____
_____
_____
_____

I cast my line out for the last time. The sun was starting to set; I could see my bobber dunking up and down. I started to reel it in...

_____
_____
_____
_____
_____
_____
_____
_____
_____
_____
_____
_____
_____
_____
_____
_____
_____
_____

As he waited for his turn he could feel the knot in his stomach tightening, every time someone was hooked up and sent on their way down the zip line.

He loved snorkeling he would live in the water if he could. he had snorkeled in the **Great Barrier Reef** dozens of times but he had never seen that kind of..

_____

_____

_____

_____

_____

_____

_____

_____

_____

_____

_____

_____

_____

_____

_____

_____

_____

_____

_____

_____

One morning you woke up to an empty house. You expected everyone to be at the breakfast table as usual. The back door was open and there was a note on the table.

_____
_____
_____
_____
_____
_____
_____
_____
_____
_____
_____
_____
_____
_____
_____
_____
_____
_____
_____
_____

You wake up alone in a forest,

with a lion cub, a note and a backpack...

_____

_____

_____

_____

_____

_____

_____

_____

_____

_____

_____

_____

_____

_____

_____

_____

_____

_____

_____

He could feel himself relax as the tires left the ground flying always brought him a sense of calm, when suddenly..

_____

_____

_____

_____

_____

_____

_____

_____

_____

_____

_____

_____

_____

_____

The perfect wave, every surfers dream when they are out on the water. I could see it coming, with it also came the worry over what happened before.

Hurrying he hooked up his dog sled team, knowing he needed to beat the storm...

_____
_____
_____
_____
_____
_____
_____
_____
_____
_____
_____
_____
_____
_____
_____
_____
_____
_____
_____

Being a river guide for a long time he had taken trips down some rough rapids in the past always managing to stay in the raft. Not this time though, it felt like someone may have pushed him out....

_____
_____
_____
_____
_____
_____
_____
_____
_____
_____
_____
_____
_____
_____
_____
_____
_____
_____

You were flying home from a trip with your best friend, when the pilot announced that there was a problem with the plane . The plane was to land immediately at the nearest airport. You found yourself in a city that you had never even heard of. The airline gave you 500 Euros each, and a hotel to stay in until the flight could be rescheduled...

_____

_____

_____

_____

_____

_____

_____

_____

_____

_____

_____

_____

_____

_____

_____

_____

Their campsite felt like it was shaking. The volcano was suppose to be dormant. It hadn't erupted in over 500 years but they could see smoke coming from the top! They had to make a plan to get to safety and quick!

_____

_____

_____

_____

_____

_____

_____

_____

_____

_____

_____

_____

_____

_____

_____

_____

Wandering the castle ruins he couldn't help but imagine about the people who lived there long ago. The vines against the wall were moving as if there was a breeze, but there was no wind, he reached inside and brushed the thick draping of vines aside to reveal a door. It was slightly ajar and he could feel a cool breeze...

_____

_____

_____

_____

_____

_____

_____

_____

_____

_____

_____

_____

_____

_____

_____

_____

_____

You had your backpack, tent, sleeping bag, food, longboard, dog, 78 dollars and a mood for adventure.

_____
_____
_____
_____
_____
_____
_____
_____
_____
_____
_____
_____
_____
_____
_____
_____
_____
_____
_____

The Forgotten Forest

The Plan...

A Boy and His Dog.

The Funniest Family Vacation.

X Marks the Spot

Storm Chasers.

Trapped!

The Lost Astronaut

Created by Estera Janisse Brown,
Melissa Knorr & Sarah Janisse Brown

Published by The Thinking Tree, LLC

Www.FunSchoolingBooks.com

Do It Yourself
HOMESCHOOL
JOURNALS

Copyright Information

Contact Us:

The Thinking Tree LLC

317.622.8852 PHONE (Dial +1 outside of the USA) 267.712.7889 FAX

FunSchoolingBooks.com

Printed in Great Britain
by Amazon